The Soap Opera *TRIVIA* QUIZ BOOK

1001 questions and answers on your favourite serials

ANTHONY HAYWARD AND
PENNY WILSON

COLUMBUS BOOKS
LONDON

First published in Great Britain in 1987 by
COLUMBUS BOOKS LIMITED
19-23 Ludgate Hill, London EC4M 7PD

British Library Cataloguing in Publication Data
Hayward, Anthony
  Soap opera trivia Quiz book.
  1. Television serials——Miscellanea
  2. Soap operas——Miscellanea
  I. Title   II. Wilson, Penny
  791.45'75   PN1992.8.S4
        ISBN 0-86287-353-3

Designed by Fred Price

Picture acknowledgements
BBC: 56, 59, 61, 71, 74, 75;
BBC Hulton Picture Library: 47, 50, 51;
National Film Archive, London:
12, 14, 15, 27, 80, 81, 88, 92, 94, 97, 103;
Scottish Television plc: 22, 24, 25.

Typeset by Cylinder Typesetting Ltd
48 Britton Street, London EC1M 5NA

Printed and bound by
The Guernsey Press
Guernsey, Channel Islands

Contents

Questions		Answers

Who Am I?

Please note that the 'Who Am I?' questions cover all the featured serials in no specific order and are placed at random through each section.

Foreword

Welcome to *The Soap Opera Trivia Quiz Book*, featuring 1001 brain-teasers on your favourite television and radio serials.

Soaps are television's biggest present-day phenomenon, but their origins go back to the 1930s and American radio, on which they were born — between soap-powder commercials. In Britain, too, such serials began on radio. Two of the most popular were *Waggoner's Walk* and *Mrs Dale's Diary* (later *The Dales*), but the top radio soap of all is *The Archers*, first broadcast in 1951 and still running.

It was almost ten years later, in December 1960, that *Coronation Street* became Britain's first television soap opera, doing for TV what stage plays such as John Osborne's *Look Back in Anger* and the films *Room at the Top* and *Saturday Night and Sunday Morning* had already done to reflect working-class life. *Coronation Street*, a contemporary drama set among ordinary people in a northern suburb, was part of a cultural revolution in the media.

Gradually the serial has changed, as society has changed, and today it is a blend of comedy and drama, biting wit and high-charged emotion. It remains the most successful soap opera, regularly attracting more viewers than any single screening of its biggest rival, *EastEnders*.

By the time *EastEnders* arrived on British television, in 1985, soap opera was already well established. *Crossroads*, which began in 1964, survived into the late 'eighties despite critical bombardment, to be given fresh life with almost a completely new cast. Another

British soap, *Emmerdale Farm,* set in the Yorkshire Dales, also continues to attract large audiences, as do the glossy American series *Dallas* and *Dynasty.* All three started in the 'seventies.

A new breed of TV serial began in 1982 with Channel Four's *Brookside,* which has always sought to portray some of the more contentious social issues, such as unemployment. *EastEnders* followed that trend and became the BBC's first big home-grown soap success. Another audience-grabber for the BBC has been *Howards' Way,* the glamour of which rivals that of the American soaps. Meanwhile *Dynasty* has spawned a spin-off, *The Colbys,* with a Californian setting. The list of British serials is completed by *Take the High Road,* set in the Scottish Highlands, which has been running since 1980.

Rivalry between the soaps makes newspaper headlines daily and helps to keep millions of people tuning in to the goings-on in their favourite TV homes. We hope this book not only creates a little real-life domestic rivalry of its own as you compete with family and friends to find the right answers, but also brings back memories of characters you have loved and loathed and events you have cherished.

For their help, we would like to thank Gervase Webb, Christine and Margaret Stewart, Nicky Manning, Steve Kingham, Donna Vine and Michael Cook.

Anthony Hayward and Penny Wilson

Questions

1 What is the name of the Ewing ranch?

2 How did Jock Ewing die?

3 In which country was the mine that Pamela Ewing invested in?

4 What was supposed to be mined there?

5 Whom did Pamela Ewing nearly marry after Bobby Ewing was presumed dead?

6 Where did he propose to her, in 1987?

7 What is the name of Jenna Wade's daughter?

8 What is the name of the Ewings' chief house-maid?

9 To whom was Bobby Ewing engaged before he supposedly died?

10 What major operation did Miss Ellie undergo while she was still married to Jock Ewing?

11 To what substance is Sue Ellen addicted?

12 With which member of her family did Pamela Ewing team up in the oil business?

13 Who was given a Porsche as her first car?

14 What was the registration number?

15 Whom were viewers led to believe that Katherine Wentworth Barnes had killed?

16 Which woman shot and nearly killed JR in 1980?

17 How was she related to Sue Ellen Ewing?

18 What was the profession of Lucy Ewing's first husband?

19 What was his name?

20 What was the name of the lingerie company that Sue Ellen Ewing launched?

21 Whom did she choose to model the new lingerie, on first setting up the company?

22 Why did she pick that particular character?

WHO AM I?

946 I am known primarily as a singer in the West End musicals, but I once appeared in *Crossroads.*

23 All smiles for Bobby and his young bride – but with whom did Pamela Ewing have an affair before she met Bobby?

24 To whom was Cliff Barnes married?

25 What is the forename of her brother?

26 How did Cliff Barnes' wife die?

27 What is the name of Pamela and Bobby Ewing's son?

28 Who is the father of Jenna Wade's second child?

29 Who was the real mother of Pamela and Bobby's Ewing's child?

30 Who was the international terrorist, wanted by the CIA, who kidnapped John Ross Ewing in 1987?

31 Who was Jock Ewing's first partner and long-standing friend in the oil business?

32 What was his nickname?

33 To what was he addicted?

34 What are the names of his children?

35 What was Miss Ellie's maiden name?

36 Who was the older brother with whom Jock Ewing fell out in his youth?

37 Who inherited the Ewing ranch when her parents died?

38 Who was Jock Ewing's first wife?

WHO AM I?

947 **I joined Britain's longest-running TV serial in 1964, became the country's best-known cleaner and won the Royal Television Society's 1984-5 Best Performance Award.**

39 What happened to her before Jock Ewing married Miss Ellie?

40 How did Miss Ellie (shown above with first husband Jock) originally persuade Jock to marry her?

41 Who 'sniffed out' Jock Ewing's first oilfields?

42 What is the name of actress Linda Gray's real-life son?

948 **We wrote the theme music for *EastEnders* and *Howards' Way*.**

43 In which city was John Ross kidnapped in 1987?

44 Sue Ellen confronts JR with another of his infidelities. But Sue Ellen herself has strayed.

What is the name of her ex-lover who was a relative of Clayton Farlow?

45 Which Ewing was elected Texas state senator in 1981?

46 Why did the first lover Sue Ellen took after marrying JR disappear from her life?

47 In which American state was Sue Ellen once crowned as a beauty queen?

48 Who was Bobby Ewing's childhood sweetheart?

49 Where did Pamela Ewing first see Bobby when he 'returned from the dead'?

50 Who was Donna Krebbs' first husband?

51 What did he do for a living?

52 Of what did he die?

53 Whom did Donna Krebbs teach after she miscarried her first child, according to her sister-in-law's dream?

54 Why did Donna and Ray Krebbs' attempt to adopt a child – in the dream – fail?

55 How was Jenna Wade affected – in the dream – by Bobby Ewing's supposed death?

56 What business was Pamela Ewing in before she joined the oil world?

57 What was the name of the company left to Pamela Ewing by her mother?

58 How did Larry Hagman make his début in show-business?

59 In which war film, based on a Jack Higgins novel and released in 1976, did Larry Hagman appear?

949 **I have played Fiona Cunningham in a Scottish serial since it began.**

60 What is Barbara Bel Geddes' real name?

61 In which year was she born?

62 In which 1950 film about a bubonic plague did she appear?

63 What was Victoria Principal before she became an actress?

64 Which *Dallas* actor's singing career faltered when musicals became unfashionable in the 1950s?

65 Who played Jamie Ewing in the serial?

66 Which *Dallas* actor starred with Ronald Reagan in the film *Prisoner of War* in 1954?

67 What annual event takes place in the grounds of the Ewing ranch?

68 Who plays Jeremy Wendell, JR Ewing's rival in the oil business?

69 Which character does Steve Kanaly play?

WHO AM I?

950 I played David Barlow in *Coronation Street* and later married an accountant in a Merseyside serial.

70 Which vital documents could not be found in Cliff Barnes' wife's safe box after she died?

71 Why was Cliff Barnes overjoyed that they were missing?

72 Who was Cliff Barnes' live-in lover before he married?

73 What was her job?

74 To which city did Donna Krebbs go when she separated from Ray Krebbs?

75 Why did she go there?

76 What is the name of JR's secretary?

77 Who were Lucy Ewing's parents?

78 In which spin-off television series did they star?

79 What major project did Ray Krebbs undertake to try to save his marriage?

WHO AM I?

951 I was in the TV series *Mrs Thursday* with Kathleen Harrison before taking the role of a vicar in a rural Yorkshire community.

80 Who persuaded Ray Krebbs to renew his friendship with Jenna Wade after his divorce from Donna?

81 What is the name of the glitzy event held annually for the Dallas oil folk?

82 Who won the Oil Man of the Year award at the 1983 ball?

83 How was his wife related to the Ewing family?

84 How did Miss Ellie find out Wes Parmalee's true identity?

85 Why was Wes Parmalee hired to work at the Ewing ranch?

86 Who shot JR Ewing in 1987 because of a business deal?

87 Where was Pamela Ewing born?

88 From what disease did the man Pamela Ewing nearly married think he was dying?

952 I left *EastEnders* after heavy publicity about my affair with a co-star who left her husband to move in with me.

89 By whom was April Stevens hired as a spy in the oil world?

90 Although April was well paid she was discontented. Why?

91 What does 'JR' stand for?

92 What is JR Ewing's personal trademark?

93 Who was the nephew whom Ray Krebbs was accused of trying to murder?

94 In which American state is Dallas?

95 In which year did *Dallas* begin?

96 Which *Dallas* actor once starred in *The Man from Atlantis* on TV?

97 In which British television show did Linda Gray and Larry Hagman appear together for the first time on Christmas Eve 1986?

98 Which two characters studied together at the University of Texas?

99 Who is Larry Hagman's actress mother?

100 What is the name of the club frequented by the major characters in *Dallas*?

Take the High Road

101 In which fictional Scottish village is *Take the High Road* set?

102 Who created *Take the High Road?*

103 What did Elizabeth Cunningham inherit when her father died?

104 Who headed the German consortium to which she sold it?

105 What is the name of the actor who played him?

106 What was the character's favourite drink?

953 I appeared in the series *Gangsters* and *The Duellists* before starring in *Howards' Way.*

107 Why did Elizabeth have to sell her house?

108 Which loch lies close to the village where the serial is set?

109 Which real loch-side village is used for filming outside scenes?

110 When was the first episode of the serial broadcast on the ITV network?

111 What is the name of Elizabeth Cunningham's former husband (shown above, with daughter Fiona)?

112 Who was his second wife?

113 What was the name of the district nurse when the serial began?

114   Who was the original minister?

115   Who succeeded him?

116   For what crime did Brian Blair serve a 10-year jail sentence?

117   Who was the country bus-driver in the serial's early days?

118   Who was the original factor of the estate?

119   Who took over from him?

120   What was Alice Taylor's maiden name?

121   How did Alice's sister die?

122   What relation had adopted son Donald been to Alice?

123   Who was Donald's father?

124   Whose orange juice was spiked with alcohol at Bob and Alice Taylor's wedding reception?

125   Why was he in the village?

WHO AM I?

> **954   I am the daughter of a famous singer (now dead) and played the character who first tried to kill JR Ewing in _Dallas_.**

126 Where did Bob and Alice honeymoon?

127 Carol McKay and Sheila Ramsay catch up on gossip. Away from the the village, the actress who plays Carol was in the film *Restless Natives*. What is her name?

128 What was the name of Brian Blair's brother?

129 What is the village's biggest annual event?

130 What is Dougal Lachlan's job?

131 From whom did Dougal break off his engagement?

132 What is Sheila Ramsay's maiden name?

133 To what was Ken Calder addicted?

134 Why did Kathleen Sneddon's parents send her to the village from Ireland?

135 What is the name of Mrs Mack's sister?

136 Who designed Sheila Ramsay's wedding dress?

137 Who was her bridesmaid?

138 Who was the father of Fiona Cunningham's baby?

139 Fergus Jamieson makes a special delivery. But who is the woman with him, who with her husband owns the village shop and post office?

140 Who operates the ferry boat?

955 I am British and I played a prisoner of war in the long-running series *Tenko* before appearing in *The Colbys*.

141 What relation was Brian Jarvis to Meg Richardson?

142 Whom did he marry?

143 Who was Meg Richardson's second husband?

144 Why did he try to murder her?

145 How did he attempt to kill her?

146 Where was he later believed to have died in an accident?

147 Who was Meg's first grandchild?

956 I appear in a Midlands soap opera, used to act in *General Hospital,* and run motor yachts as a hobby.

148 Who were the parents?

149 What was the name of David Hunter's first wife?

150 Who became pregnant by David Hunter while he was married to his second wife?

151 What was the name of the actress who played her?

152 Where did Adam and Jill Chance (above) honeymoon?

153 Whom did they meet there?

154 How was the motel destroyed in 1981?

155 How was it destroyed in 1967?

156 Where did Meg and the staff spend a working holiday while the motel was being rebuilt in 1967?

157 What was the name of Vernon Daintry's wife?

158 Who designed the motel's new reception area in 1985?

159 In what capacity did Daniel Freeman join the motel?

160 Which *Crossroads* actor played surgeon Andrew Shaw in *Emergency – Ward 10?*

161 What was Violet Blundell's job at the motel?

162 What did she leave to do?

163 Who won the 1985 motel beauty contest?

164 Who was disqualified after originally being named winner?

165 Which of Meg's husbands was kidnapped?

166 How did he die?

167 What is Benny's surname?

168 For what did waitress Marilyn Gates leave her job in 1966?

169 Whom did she marry, in 1968?

957   I play a major part in *EastEnders* and am fascinated by frogs, which I collect.

170 Whom did Andy Fraser marry in 1966?

171 To whom did Meg become engaged in 1965 but not marry until 10 years later?

172 Why did he break off the engagement in 1968?

173 What was the name of the stage, TV and film actor who played him?

174 Of what crime was Brian Jarvis accused in 1968?

175 What was the name of Sid Hooper's first wife?

176 Actor Norman Bowler played the local newspaper editor. What was the name of his character?

177 What was the name of Stephen Fellowes' housekeeper?

178 Which former *Crossroads* actress is married to ex-singer Carl Wayne?

179 What was the name of the character she played?

180 To whom was Kath Brownlow engaged before marrying Stephen Fellowes?

958 I appeared in *Brookside* as Lisa, a girlfriend of Pat Hancock; in another serial I worked in a battery-hen unit then became unemployed.

181 What was the name of the boss who sacked Kevin Banks as a sportswear salesman?

182 Arthur White, who played the boss, is the brother of which comedy actor?

183 What did Roy Lambert do before becoming a motel garage mechanic?

184 Who returned to the motel to advise Jill Chance when share transfers were being discussed in 1985?

185 Of what did Jane Templeton die?

186 How and where did chef Carlos Raphael die in 1969?

187 What was the name of the man Jill Richardson married bigamously in 1970?

188 How did he die?

189 Whom did Jill marry in 1971?

190 What was his job?

959 **I once had a mastectomy — an event the *Dallas* scriptwriters wrote into the part I play.**

191 Whom did motel manager Paul Stevens marry?

192 Who played Paul Stevens?

193 Who played Sandra Gould?

194 What was David Hunter's first job at the motel, in 1971?

195 What was the name of Diane Lawton's first husband?

196 What was his job?

197 What was the name of Diane's son?

198 Who was his father?

199 When his father kidnapped him, where did he take him?

200 Whom did Sheila Harvey marry?

201 Of what did Wilf Harvey die?

202 What was Benny's first job in the serial?

203 With whom did David Hunter have an affair in 1975?

204 What was her job?

205 Who was raped in 1976?

206 Whom was Benny due to marry in 1977?

207 Why did the wedding not go ahead?

208 To what did David Hunter become addicted?

209 Who helped him to beat it?

210 By whom did Jill Harvey have a son in 1977?

211 What relation was the father to her?

212 What was the name of the son?

213 Whom did Diane Parker marry in 1979?

214 Why was Paul Ross attacked in 1985?

215 Whom was Benny suspected of murdering in 1979?

216 Who shot David Hunter in 1980?

217 Why?

218 How was Arthur Brownlow killed?

219 What was the name of Glenda and Kevin Banks' daughter?

220 What was unusual about her?

WHO AM I?

960 I played Monica Downes in *The Archers,* Nurse Ford in *Emergency—Ward 10* and spoke the first words in another long-running television soap opera.

221 What was the original idea for the title of *Crossroads*?

222 Who led a petition to save *Crossroads* when it was dropped in the London ITV region in 1968?

223 What was the name of the motel's original, Spanish chef?

224 What was the name of the motel's Scottish chef?

225 Which *Crossroads* actress (above) was in the film *Gregory's Girl*?

226 What is the name of her *Crossroads* character?

227 From whom did the character break off her engagement?

228 What was his job at the time?

229 Who succeeded Adam Chance as manager of the motel leisure centre?

230 What relation was he to Nicola Freeman?

231 Who taught Benny to read?

232 How was Benny temporarily blinded?

233 How many children did Sam Benson have?

234 What was Adam Chance's first job at the motel?

235 In what capacity did Mr Darby join the motel?

236 To which city did Kath and Stephen Fellowes move?

237 What was Glenda Brownlow's job at the motel?

238 A *Crossroads* actor appeared in the acclaimed stage play *Another Country*. Who was the actor and what was the name of his character?

WHO AM I?

961 At 11 I appeared in *Upstairs, Downstairs;* I was later 'seduced' by David Bowie in Brecht's play *Baal* and left *Howards' Way* after the second series.

239 Who taught Diane Hunter to shoot?

240 What was the name of Nicola Freeman's illegitimate daughter?

241 Who was Nicola's brother?

242 After arriving at the motel, with whom did he have an affair?

243 Whom did Adam Chance accuse of stealing a pendant?

244 What was her job?

245 What was the name of Kath Fellowes's son by her first marriage?

246 Why did he leave the motel?

247 What was the name of Daniel Freeman's twin sister?

248 Where did Sid Hooper work after being made redundant from the motel garage?

WHO AM I?

> **962** I appeared in *Coronation Street* and *Follyfoot* before playing an auctioneer who once had an illegitimate baby that was adopted.

249 Gian Sammarco, star of the *Adrian Mole* TV series, played a nasty schoolboy in *Crossroads*. What was his name?

250 What did the schoolboy do to Benny's dog?

251 What was the name of the dog?

252 Who blackmailed Nicola Freeman?

253 What did he threaten to do?

254 What was the name of Nicola Freeman's aristocratic friend?

255 What was the name of the old schoolfriend of Nicola Freeman who used the motel's leisure centre?

256 Who arrived from New Orleans in 1986 to help to run the motel while Jill Chance was in hospital with pregnancy complications?

257 Which now-famous singer played Caroline Winthrop?

258 What is Tommy Lancaster's nickname?

259 What is the name of the former *Softly, Softly* actor who plays him?

260 What are the names of Alexis Colby's three former husbands?

261 Which member of her family did Alexis discover in bed with Dex Dexter?

262 Why did Alexis marry Cecil Colby?

263 Where did Amanda Carrington once try to commit suicide?

264 Whom did she try to contact to save her?

265 What is the name of Blake Carrington's brother?

266 What was the major business deal that brought together Alexis and her three former husbands in 1986?

267 What was the forename of the woman who impersonated Krystle Carrington after she was kidnapped?

268 In which country did Ben Carrington go to live when he left America?

269 Who went there to persuade him to return to America?

270 What is the name of Krystle Carrington's daughter?

271 Who started the fire at La Mirage?

272 How did it start?

273 Where did Claudia Blaisdel and Adam Carrington get married?

274 What was Michael Culhane's job?

275 Whom did Michael once try to drown?

276 What is the name of Alexis' newspaper?

277 Why did Dominique Devereaux break off her engagement to Garrett Boyston?

278 What is the forename of Garrett Boyston's common-law wife?

279 Who ended up in hospital with serious burns after the La Mirage fire?

963 I played a Borchester Technical College student aiming to work in fashion or the media. Then I joined a serial about a motel.

280 Who is her father?

281 Who discovered Amanda Carrington and Clay Fallmont kissing near a pool?

282 Who played that character's father?

283 Of what did he die in real life?

284 What major gift did Sammy Jo give Clay Fallmont's mother, Emily?

285 Who tried to poison Blake Carrington in 1986?

286 Which member of his family was Blake Carrington accused of murdering?

287 What is the name of Steven Carrington's son?

288 In which spin-off TV serial does lawyer Garrett Boyston appear?

289 What was Blake Carrington's old company called?

290 Which company did he then form?

WHO AM I?

964 **Although I play an alcoholic wife in an American soap, in real life I am a health fanatic and steer clear of scandal and headlines.**

291 What was Blake Carrington's main aim when he formed that company?

292 Who kidnapped Steven Carrington's son?

293 What relation was Claudia Blaisdel to Steven Carrington's son?

294 How is Caresse Morelle related to Alexis?

295 In which country was Caresse Morelle jailed?

296 In which city was the jail?

297 How long did Caresse Morelle spend in jail?

298 What was Alexis' main complaint against Caresse Morelle?

299 In which country did Amanda Carrington spend most of her childhood?

300 What was the name of the hotel to which Blake and Krystle Carrington moved after they left their home?

301 Who forced them to move out of their home so that she could live there?

302 Which two characters had a fight over Blake Carrington that resulted in their sliding down a muddy hill?

303 What is the name of Blake Carrington's half-sister?

304 What is the name of the hotel owned by Blake Carrington?

305 Who was the hotel manager before it burned down?

306 What was Adam Carrington's profession before he joined the family business?

307 What relation is Sammy Jo to Krystle Carrington?

308 What is the name of Sammy Jo's ranch?

309 What does she do for a living on the ranch?

310 In which colours is the exterior of the Carrington house painted?

311 Who told Ben Carrington to get out of Alexis' life and home after he returned from abroad?

312 Who plays Blake Carrington?

313 In which city is the Carrington house?

314 Where is the serial made?

315 What was the name of Steven Carrington's boy-friend?

965 I played the mother of Billy Liar in the TV production and later took the role of a motel housekeeper.

316 In which fictional country did Steven Carrington's boyfriend die?

317 Whom did Dex Dexter rescue in that country?

318 What did that person pretend he was suffering from?

319 Before Jeff Colby renewed his relationship with Fallon Colby, he fell in love with Lady Ashley Cooper. What was her job?

320 Who played Lady Ashley Cooper?

321 What is the name of Ben Carrington's young niece?

322 With whom did Amanda Carrington begin living against her father's wishes?

323 Who played Joel Abrigore, who kidnapped Krystle Carrington?

324 After which character has a perfume been named?

325 Who rescued Caresse Morelle from prison?

966 I appeared regularly in *Grange Hill* before becoming a teenage mother in another serial set in East London.

326 Who plays Caresse Morelle?

327 During the filming of her rescue from prison, what did the actress who plays Caresse Morelle refuse to do?

328 Who organized the rescue of Caresse Morelle from prison?

329 Why was he so eager to rescue her?

330 By whom did Sammy Jo Carrington become pregnant with her second child?

331 Where were they when Sammy Jo told him that she was pregnant?

332 Who was responsible for sending Caresse Morelle to prison?

333 Who played the original Fallon Colby?

334 What was Caresse Morelle's job on Alexis' newspaper?

335 How did Krystle get her name?

WHO AM I?

967 I was Norma Ford in *Coronation Street* and later became a secretary for NY Estates in a rural soap opera.

336 What did Blake Carrington's mother leave him when she died?

337 What type of car does Ben Carrington drive?

338 What was the forename of the woman Caresse Morelle tried to blackmail over an affair with Ben Carrington?

339 Who paid the blackmail money?

340 Where did Alexis find the ring with which Dex Dexter proposed marriage to her for the second time?

341 Where was Krystle kept prisoner after she was kidnapped?

342 Which member of the Carrington family was involved in her kidnapping?

343 To which Carrington was this character married?

344 What is Caresse Morelle's nickname?

345 With what was Blake Carrington charged after the fire at La Mirage?

968 I am a famous screen star, and I moved from films to television to play Jason in *The Colbys*.

346 How much money did Alexis offer as a reward for information leading to the capture and arrest of the person who started the La Mirage fire?

347 Who plays Dex Dexter?

348 Who played the Prince of Moldavia?

349 In which year was Joan Collins born?

350 What are the names of the two soft-porn films (1978 and 1979) in which she starred?

351 Who designs the *Dynasty* clothes and is famous for the rebirth of the shoulder pad?

352 Who plays Krystle Carrington?

353 Which TV mini-series did she film in the Australian outback in 1986?

354 Who plays Adam Carrington?

355 Who acted as a front man in buying shares for Michael Culhane in Blake Carrington's new company?

356 Against whom did Joan Collins start real-life divorce proceedings in 1986?

357 One *Dynasty* actor provided the voice for Charlie in the American television series *Charlie's Angels*. Who was it?

358 Which of Blake Carrington's employees in his new company turned out to have been an old schoolfriend of Adam Carrington?

359 Which member of the Carrington family worked for Blake Carrington in order to spy for Alexis?

The Archers

360 In what fictional county is Ambridge?

361 What is the name of the local newspaper?

362 Where does Jennifer Aldridge live?

363 Where does John Tregorran live?

364 What was the name of Jethro Larkin's dog?

365 Dan Archer (Harry Oakes) and Tom Forrest (Bob Arnold) deep in conversation. But why did Tom eventually put away his guns?

366 Who owns Grey Gables Country Club?

367 Of what is he also a director?

368 Which river runs through Ambridge?

369 When did Doris Archer die?

370 How old was she?

371 What was Dan Archer doing when he died?

372 What is the name of the bitter served in the Bull?

373 For which darts team does Eddie Grundy play?

374 With whom did Brian Aldridge have an affair in 1986?

375 How did *The Archers* try to divert attention from ITV's opening night, in 1955?

376 What is Sergeant Dave Barrett's hobby?

377 In what period was the farmhouse at Brookfield built?

969 **I replaced the original Miss Ellie in *Dallas* for a brief period while she was indisposed.**

378 What is the name of the mid-Victorian villa that has gardens running down to the river?

379 What is the name of Shula Archer's twin brother?

380 To whom did David Archer get engaged in 1986?

381 Which actor, who died in 1984, played the original Joe Grundy?

382 Who is Portia?

383 To which saint is the parish church of Ambridge dedicated?

384 Who is chairman of the parish council?

385 Who captains the Bull's darts team?

386 Which political party does Mark Hebden represent on the council?

387 What is Eddie Grundy's hobby?

388 What is the name of the chef at Grey Gables?

389 Who moved into Ambridge Hall after Col. Freddie Danby was forced to move out?

390 Who played the original Doris Archer?

391 What did Col. Freddie Danby call his duck pen?

392 Who discovered a Civil War stone cannonball in the roots of a dead laurel bush?

393 What does he use it as?

394 Life was busy for Dan Archer (shown above with Len Thomas) as a farmer before he retired. What was his farm called?

395 Who left the house to Doris in her will?

396 Where were three Bronze Age barrows found?

397 Who lives in Honeysuckle Cottage?

398 Who disrupted the 1987 Parish Council elections by standing as an environmentalist (for the Green Party)?

399 Who was Dan Archer's father?

400 Who was the last actor to play Dan?

401 What did Ambridge garage used to be?

402 Who were the last owners of it in that form?

403 What was Doris Archer's maiden name?

404 Who were her parents?

405 A leisurely country walk for Dan and Doris Archer. On what date did they marry?

406 With what major crime was Nelson Gabriel implicated in the 1960s?

407 Who is Ambridge's oldest inhabitant?

408 What is the name of the local regiment?

409 Which couple were the first to start farming organically in Ambridge?

410 Who took the photographs at Shula Archer's wedding?

411 Who runs the village shop?

412 Who is landlord of the Bull?

413 What was the name of his late wife?

414 How did she die?

415 Who is the most famous Ambridge ghost?

416 Where does he appear at midnight on Lady Day (25 March)?

417 Which female member of the Royal Family has taken part in the serial?

970 **I played Susan Cunningham in the first episode of _Coronation Street_.**

418 Who has played Phil Archer since the first episode of *The Archers*?

419 Who is the local doctor?

420 Who was previously Ambridge's doctor, who lived in the village?

421 Where are the old folk's bungalows?

422 What was Doris Archer's first job, in 1914?

423 To what type of school did David Archer go?

424 Where was there an outbreak of food poisoning during Christmas 1986?

425 What caused it?

426 What is the name of *The Archers'* theme tune?

427 Which character went to work in the City when the original actor left to join *Crossroads*?

428 What is the nearest railway station to Ambridge?

429 What was the name of Phil Archer's first wife?

971 Nine years after playing Catriona in the film of Robert Louis Stevenson's book *Kidnapped*, I played Kay Grant in *Take the High Road*.

430 How did she die?

431 Which character did the late Ted Moult play?

432 For which ice-cream firm did Nigel Pargetter work?

433 What was Lester Nicholson's job?

434 Who was his wife?

435 What anniversary did *The Archers* celebrate on 1 January 1986?

436 Who jilted Eddie Grundy on the eve of his wedding in 1979?

437 Why was Eddie barred from the Bull by Sid Perks?

438 Who farms Home Farm?

439 Who runs the Ambridge playgroup?

440 What is the name of the fictional London borough in which *EastEnders* is set?

441 What brand of cigarettes does Mehmet Osman smoke?

442 Which *EastEnders* character's voice can be heard on British Telecom's Soapline?

443 Who dressed up as Santa at Christmas 1986?

444 Which roles did Lofty and Michelle Holloway take in the 1986 Christmas nativity play?

445 Where did Angie and Sharon Watts go to live when Den announced he was filing for divorce?

446 Where is *EastEnders* recorded?

447 Who is the series producer?

448 What ailment does Lofty suffer from?

449 What was the title of actor Nick Berry's hit single?

450 How old did Kelvin Carpenter become on his birthday in January 1987?

451 What is the pub's full name?

452 Who played the part of Den's mistress Jan?

453 What is the name of actor Leonard Winger's (Eddie Hunter's) real-life band in London?

454 What was in the lethal cocktail mixed for Lofty's stag night?

455 Which organization did Kathy Beale join as a volunteer?

456 Who is the father of Michelle's baby?

457 What are the names of the two dogs in *East-Enders?*

458 Kathy and Pete Beale have not always looked so happy: who blackmailed Kathy when he found out she had been raped as a teenager and had to give her baby up for adoption?

459 What was the name of Lou Beale's husband?

460 What was the name of Naima Jeffery's husband?

461 Who bought Michelle's motorbike as a present for their son?

462 Why did actor Peter Dean (Pete Beale) give up smoking in real life?

463 How did Arthur Fowler get the money to pay for Michelle's wedding?

464 Who moved into Debbie Wilkins' house when she sold it?

465 To which fictional TV character does Susan Osman liken her brother-in-law, Mehmet?

466 Who plays Lofty Holloway?

467 What is the name of Wicksy's mother?

468 What is the name of Nick Cotton's mother?

469 What crime did Nick commit against his mother?

972 I am the sister of Brian Rix and play a matriarchal figure in a rural serial.

470 Where did Lofty and Michelle Holloway marry at the second attempt?

471 What famous train trip did Den book as a surprise for Angie in Venice?

472 What was the name of actor Leslie Grantham's real-life brother, who died in 1986?

473 Of what disorder did he die?

474 Why was Leslie Grantham jailed in Germany in 1967?

475 What was the name of the *EastEnders* band?

476 What was the title of the band's real-life hit single?

477 Who plays Pat Wicks?

478 What relation is Pete Beale to Pauline Fowler?

479 Who is Wicksy's real father?

480 From which country did Andy O'Brien originate?

481 How did he die?

482 With what colour was Andy's coffin lined?

483 What were Debbie's last words to Andy before he died?

484 Who is the father of Mary Smith's child?

485 What is the name of Mary's child?

486 What bet did Mehmet Osman make with Ali over Mary?

487 Who 'burgled' the Fowlers' house?

488 Of what nationality are Mehmet and Ali Osman?

489 What was the name of Ali and Sue's son?

490 How did Ali and Sue's son die?

491 Arthur and Pauline are the proud parents of three children. For what crime was their son Mark imprisoned?

492 For how long did Jan and Den have an affair?

493 How did Mary try to ruin Ali's taxi firm?

494 What is the name of Ali's taxi firm?

495 What is its telephone number?

496 What disease did Angie tell Den she was suffering from to stop him leaving her?

497 With which member of the *EastEnders* cast did actress Linda Davidson (Mary Smith) begin a romance in real life?

498 What is Wicksy's forename?

499 Where did Michelle and Lofty go for their honeymoon?

500 With whom did Tony Carpenter have a short affair?

501 To which country did Tony buy an air ticket after splitting up with his wife for the second time?

502 What is Carmel Roberts' job?

WHO AM I?

973 **I acted in the films *Yanks* and *Chariots of Fire* and had four roles in *Coronation Street* and two in *Emmerdale Farm* before becoming a regular in a Liverpool-based serial, in which I ran a part-time catering business for a while.**

503 Why was Ethel Skinner admitted to hospital?

504 Dot Cotton is always talking about her estranged husband. What is his name?

505 On what charge did Dot appear in court?

506 What is Dr Legg's first name?

507 What was the title of the hit single recorded by actress Anita Dobson (Angie Watts) and the Simon May Orchestra?

508 Who shared a celebratory drink with Den when his divorce was finalized?

509 Whom did James Willmott-Brown ask to oversee the workmen refurbishing his pub?

510 What was the name of Hannah Carpenter's boyfriend after she split up with Tony for the first time?

511 How many jumpers did Kathy Beale knit in one night, with Michelle Holloway's help, when first commissioned by Mehmet Osman?

512 Who was Ian Beale's first girlfriend?

513 What reason does Dot give for her 'hot flushes'?

514 Who is the cleaner at Dr Legg's office?

515 Why did Michelle leave Lofty at the altar first time round?

974 I starred in *The Forgotten Voyage*, *A Family Affair* and *Second Choice* before joining *Howards' Way*.

516 Who found Angie when she attempted suicide?

517 Of what substances did Angie take an overdose?

518 Whom do Naima Jeffery's parents want her to marry?

519 What did Mary turn to for extra money, with the help of Pat Wicks?

520 Who beat Mary up?

521 For which career did Michelle Holloway once train?

522 Who once persuaded Mary Smith to dye her hair back to its natural colour?

523 Why did Wicksy quit the band before the 1986 music contest?

524 What does Dot Cotton always drink at the pub?

525 Where was 1986's much-talked-about talent contest held?

WHO AM I?

975 I played Vera Hopkins in *Coronation Street*, Winnie Purvis in *Emmerdale Farm* and Doris Luke in *Crossroads*. Some people think I'm batty.

526 With whom did Colin Russell begin an affair after he moved to the Square?

527 What scheme did Sharon join after she quit school?

528 What did Tony Carpenter find on his fence the morning after Kelvin's birthday party?

529 What did Kathy Beale take up at home to make extra money?

530 With whom did Ethel Skinner move in after she was discharged from hospital?

531 With whom did Debbie share a flat after selling her house?

532 Who anonymously sent the Fowler family £20 through the post?

533 What was Ian Beale's major hang-up before he met girlfriend Tina?

534 Whom did Den take with him to his first meeting with Sharon after he filed for divorce from Angie?

WHO AM I?

976 **In our TV roles we played mother, son and daughter and ran a family business together in the Midlands.**

535 Why did Dot Cotton disapprove of the doctor who replaced Dr Legg shortly after Christmas 1986?

536 How did Den find out that Angie was not dying on their trip back from Venice?

537 What did Dot Cotton win in a pop music competition?

538 What did Sharon give Barry to sell for her?

539 What was Jan's job when she was first seen in the serial?

540 What was the nationality of the man who met Jan in Venice and wanted to marry her?

541 Where did Debbie go to work after Andy's death?

542 Who redecorated that place?

543 Which member of the Carpenter family went to live with Hannah when she left Tony?

WHO AM I?

977 I appear in *Howards' Way* and, in 1986, was reported to be having an affair with co-star Tracey Childs (Lynne Howard).

544 What did Kelvin do in the laundrette that Dot didn't approve of before his wild birthday party?

545 Which two women work in the laundrette?

546 Who called the police to Kelvin's birthday party because of the noise?

547 What were Kelvin's parents planning to do at mid-night during his birthday party?

548 Of what did Michelle accuse Lofty during their first fight after they married?

549 What is the name of Ali and Sue's café?

550 Why did Michelle say she had called her baby Vicki?

551 In which month of 1986 was baby Vicki born?

552 How did Pauline Fowler find out that Den Watts was Vicki's father?

978 I was born in East Kilbride, appeared on TV in *The Prime of Miss Jean Brodie* and *Maggie*, and in the film *Gregory's Girl* — for which I won the Royal Variety Club's award for Best Film Actress of 1981 — before taking the role of a motel receptionist.

553 What does Colin Russell do for a living?

554 What does Pete Beale sell on his stall?

555 What is the name of the rival pub in *EastEnders*?

556 Where does Pete Beale's brother live?

557 What does Mary Smith often wear in her nose?

558 With what gift did Den present Sharon when he met her for the first time after he filed for his divorce from Angie?

559 What was Dot Cotton afraid of when the doctor prescribed hormonal treatment for her depression?

560 Of what did Naima Jeffery become a supporter after her divorce?

561 What group did she join?

562 Who plays the part of Pauline's mother Lou?

563 In what capacity did Ali want Naima to join his taxi firm?

564 Who was the first person Mary Smith told about her being beaten up in early 1987?

565 What did Lofty give Michelle to make up for the first fight of their marriage?

566 Which *EastEnders* actress left her husband to move in with actor Ross Davidson (Andy O'Brien) in real life?

567   Where did the BBC find Vicki when searching for a baby to act as Michelle's?

568   What did a strange sign that suddenly appeared in the laundrette prohibit?

569   What was actor Peter Dean's job before he was cast in *EastEnders* as Pete Beale?

570   Who refused to lend Naima Jeffery tools with which to fix her leaking roof?

571   What did Lou Beale have stolen in the Fowlers' 'burglary'?

572   What does Angie often call her make-up?

573   Why was Arthur Fowler taken to hospital?

574   What is the name of actor Leslie Grantham's real-life actress wife?

575   Which former *Coronation Street* scriptwriter joined *EastEnders*?

576   Who plays Wicksy?

577   Which *EastEnders* actress was reported to have been having an affair with actor Tom Watt off the *EastEnders* set?

578   Who plays the part of Sharon?

579   What colour was the outfit worn by Michelle when Lofty announced to the pub that they were officially engaged?

580 What stone was set in the ring given by Lofty to Michelle for their engagement?

581 Why does no one listen to Dot Cotton's health complaints?

582 What musical instrument does James Willmott-Brown play?

583 Where did Angie spot Jan and Den together in Venice?

584 What is so unusual in television about the beer served on the set of the Queen Vic?

585 What sort of earring does Mary Smith usually wear?

586 Why did Mary Smith go for a spell without any make-up?

587 What did Andy teach Mary?

588 Is Roly male or female?

589 Who raised the alarm after finding Pat Wicks beaten up in the park?

979 I play an East London character who attempted suicide and tried to save her marriage by booking a holiday in Venice.

HOWARDS'
WAY

590 What is the serial's nickname inside the BBC?

591 With which co-star was actress Jan Harvey reported to be having a real-life affair in 1986?

592 Who is the serial's producer?

593 Who are Abi's parents?

594 What was the original idea for the serial's title?

595 What is the name of the fictional town in which the serial is set?

596 Who is Tom Howards' business partner?

597 Where is *Howards' Way* filmed?

598 Who is Abi's real father?

599 Whom did Lynne Howard marry?

600 What was his job?

601 Who is Jan Howard's oldest friend?

602 What is the nationality of Abi's baby's father?

603 Who owns Jan Howard's boutique?

604 Tom Howard and Avril Rolfe make a happy couple, but with whom did Avril have an affair before she met Tom?

605 What does Avril's father suffer from?

606 Who designed Lynne's wedding dress?

607 What relation is Kate Howard to Jan?

608 Which character always wore his hair in a ponytail?

609 What is the name of the local pub?

610 From what did Lynne suffer after she discovered Charles Frere in bed with his wife?

611 Who desperately wanted to marry Jan?

612 Which hymn was played at Lynne's wedding?

613 Who plays the part of Tom Howard?

614 Who is the father of Abi's baby?

615 What happened to the baby?

616 What is the name of the boatyard?

617 Who is the singer on the hit single 'Always There', based on the serial's theme tune?

WHO AM I?

980 **In real life I am the former wife of a pop singer whose death in 1975 was mourned worldwide.**

618   Where does Jack Rolfe keep his wellington boots?

619   Who plays the part of Kate Howard?

620   Why did Kate's first attempt to get out of financial trouble fail?

621   At the end of the second series the actress who plays Kate was living with her daughter. Why?

622   Who was sent to America to meet Lynne after she had sailed across the Atlantic?

623   What was the name of the Howard family's boat when the series began?

624   What was the name of the first non-wooden boat to be built at the yard?

625   What was it made of?

626   With what sort of pressure group did Leo become involved to fight Charles Frere's land-development plans?

981   I play an *Archers* character who always sees farming as a business and often says he has no time for starry-eyed, woolly conservationists.

627 Charles Frere, self-assured as ever: but who bribed him to drop one of his plans to develop land in the town?

628 Why did his plan fail?

629 Who was financially crippled by Charles Frere's decision to pull out of the deal?

630 What was Leo Howard's first part-time job after leaving college?

631 At which racecourse did Jan Howard's mother and Jack Rolfe spend much of their time together?

632 How did Claude Dupont die?

633 Where was Claude Dupont due to be later that day?

634 What caused Jan Howard and Ken Masters to split up towards the end of the second series?

635 What was the *Barracuda* renamed after Lynne sailed it across the Atlantic?

636 Why was Tom Howard forced to mortgage his house?

637 Who was Ken Masters' favourite pop singer?

638 Where did the affair between Ken Masters and Jan Howard first blossom?

639 In which city did Abi live with her child after returning from abroad?

982 **My brother is actor and comedian Duggie Brown. I appeared in the film *Kes* and, as a character in a northern soap opera, I am a widow and have a grandson called Nicky.**

640 What was Billy Walker's first job after National Service?

641 Who was left in Blackpool after a coach trip to the illuminations?

642 Who were the happy couple at the *Street*'s first wedding?

643 Who took over as Rover's Return barmaid when Concepta Riley married in 1961?

644 What was Valerie Barlow's hairdressing shop called?

983 I played Nigel Pargetter in *The Archers* before playing the assistant manager of a motel.

645 Who bought Leonard Swindley's Gamma Garments business?

646 Who was the snake-dancer girlfriend with whom Dennis Tanner went to London?

647 What was the name of the actress who played her?

648 Who had a nervous breakdown and was talked down from the roof of the raincoat factory by Ken Barlow after being jilted by her plumber boyfriend?

649 What is Curly Watts's real forename?

650 What was the forename of Bet Lynch's illegitimate son?

651 How did he die?

652 Mark Eden, who plays Alan Bradley, once portrayed another character, a boyfriend of Elsie Tanner. What was this character's name?

WHO AM I?

984   **I'm British, have a teenaged daughter called Katy and a sister who writes best-selling novels.**

653 Who was driving when Martin Platt was injured in a car accident?

654 How old was she then?

655 Whose car was she driving?

656 What type of contest had she just won?

657 Who broke into Alf Roberts' shop and stole bottles of alcohol?

658 How much was the alcohol worth?

659 What did he want the alcohol for?

660 Who was the first producer of *Coronation Street*?

661 One of the *Street*'s best-loved actresses died of lung cancer in 1986. Who was she, and what was the name of the character she played?

662 To which building were *Street* residents evacuated when there was a gas emergency in 1961?

663 Who was its caretaker?

664 What was the name of the late actress who played her?

665 From whom did Florrie Lindley buy the corner shop when the serial started?

666 What was the name of Florrie's husband?

667 With whom did Florrie have an affair?

668 Who performed the official opening of the new outdoor *Street* set in 1982?

669 In which fictional Manchester suburb is *Coronation Street* set?

670 On which real-life street was the serial based?

671 Who were Ken Barlow's parents?

672 From what job did Ken's father retire?

673 Who moved in with Mike Baldwin shortly after he arrived in *Coronation Street*?

674 Mike Baldwin and Emily seem to have a slight problem: what is his factory called?

675 What was the name of the ex-boyfriend who tried to woo back Gloria Todd when he was released from jail?

676 Who played hippie commune leader Robert Croft?

677 How did Ken Barlow pay for his first wedding?

678 From where did Susan Barlow's brother, Peter, come to attend her wedding to Mike Baldwin?

679 Why did Ken Barlow object to Susan's marriage?

680 The ladies of the *Street* discuss a problem over a drink. Doris Speed (Annie Walker) can be seen standing on the right: which character (not pictured) staged a *This Is Your Life* presentation for Annie Walker in 1963?

681 To whom did Emily Nugent make a Leap Year proposal in 1964?

682 Who gave Valerie Barlow piano lessons?

683 When Ken and Valerie Barlow threw a fancy-dress party, whom did Annie Walker go as?

684 Who dug Ena Sharples out of the debris when a train careered over the viaduct and into the street?

685 Which aristocrat appeared in the serial when the *Street* characters went on a coach trip to Woburn?

686 What was Jerry Booth's trade?

687 Of what did he die, in 1975?

688 Whose baby did Terry Duckworth father?

689 What was her father's forename?

690 What was his job?

985 I played Florrie Lindley in the early days of *Coronation Street* and Edna Cross in *Brookside*.

691 From whom did he buy his family's house in the street?

692 To what was Les Clegg addicted?

693 What was the name of his wife?

694 What was their son's name?

695 What is the name of his real mother?

696 Why did the Cleggs adopt him?

697 Whom did Les Clegg's wife marry after their divorce?

698 What was the name of David and Irma Barlow's son?

699 How did David and his son die?

700 Who were Irma Barlow's parents?

701 Where was Irma's first job?

702 To whom was Billy Walker briefly engaged in 1975?

986 In 1986, my parents were shot dead in their bar in Boulder, Montana, by two teenagers for a bottle of whisky and $90 cash.

703 For what was Ken Barlow jailed in 1967?

704 Who had a fight in the Rover's with Ken over an article he subsequently wrote for a left-wing review, *Survival*, reprinted in the *Manchester Evening News*?

705 Who was Ken's second wife?

706 With whom, and where, did Ken's twin children stay after their mother, Valerie, died?

707 How was Albert Tatlock related to Ken?

708 Who was best man at Dennis Tanner and Jenny Sutton's wedding?

709 What was Rita Fairclough's maiden name?

710 Who was Rita's agent in her singing days?

711 What is the name of the actor who played him?

712 What was the character's job at the time of the Rover's fire in 1986?

987 **After writing *Grange Hill*, I created *Brookside*.**

713 Whom did Sheila Birtles marry, in 1967?

714 What was the forename of the man whom Suzie Birchall married and who beat her up?

715 Mike Baldwin once owned a shop that sold denims. What was it called?

716 What business did Emily and Ernest Bishop run together?

717 How did they meet?

718 What was Emily's maiden name?

719 Who won a car in a Best Husband competition in 1986?

720 Which Army regiment did Terry Duckworth join as a trainee in 1982?

721 In what street is the late Len Fairclough's yard?

722 Who was Len's first wife?

723 What was the name of their son?

988 I played Gordon Clegg in *Coronation Street* and have since become a theatrical impresario.

724 Who was the actor, later to become lead singer of a famous pop group, who played the Faircloughs' son?

725 What was the name of Len and Rita Fairclough's foster daughter?

726 Whom did she try to seduce?

727 From which street did Fred Gee move when he became resident bar/cellarman at the Rover's?

728 Who sacked Fred from the Rover's in 1984?

729 Whom did Elsie Tanner leave the *Street* to join in a new life in Portugal?

730 What was his naval rank?

731 Whom did Christine Hardman marry?

732 How did he die?

733 To whom did Christine then become engaged briefly?

989 I played Jamie Barnes, JR's long-lost cousin, in *Dallas*.

734 What was the name of Harry Hewitt's second wife?

735 What was their son's name?

736 What was the name of Harry's daughter, who lodged at the Rover's?

737 What was Martha Longhurst's job?

738 How and where did she die?

739 What was the name of Deirdre Barlow's mother?

740 Who was Deirdre's first husband?

741 What was her job when she married him?

742 What was the name of the waitress with whom Deirdre's first husband had an affair?

743 What is Bet Lynch's position at the Rover's?

744 What was the name of the railway-enthusiast lodger Hilda Ogden took in after the death of her husband Stan?

990 I am the actress who originally played Alexis' long-lost daughter in *Dynasty*. My real-life mother is Princess Elizabeth of Yugoslavia.

745 Stan was rumoured to have a romantic interest in a woman on his window-cleaning round. At what address did she live?

746 Where did Mavis Riley and Emily Bishop work together?

747 More problems for the lovelorn Mavis, it seems. But who was her first love in the *Street*?

748 What was Mavis's job before working at the Kabin?

749 What is the name of Mavis's budgerigar?

750 How many times has Alf Roberts been married?

751 Name the wives.

752 What relation is his present wife to Gail Tilsey?

753 What was Gail's maiden name?

754 Which *Street* character's 'trademark' was her hairnet?

755 What was her husband's name?

756 What was the name of Brian Tilsley's cousin, with whom Gail had an affair?

757 In which country did Gail's lover live before coming to England?

758 Why did Brian walk out on Gail?

759 With which character did Gail first arrive in the *Street*?

760 Where did they work initially?

761 What is the name of the café Gail runs?

762 What was Annie Walker's maiden name?

763 From where did her family come?

991 I wrote the theme music for *Crossroads* and *Emmerdale Farm.*

764   To which town did Annie move after leaving the Rover's?

765   With whom does she live?

766   Who won £3,500 as a result of Curly Watts' racing tips?

767   What is the name of Kevin Webster's sister?

768   Where did Kevin's family move on to after leaving Southampton?

769   What was Sally Webster's maiden name?

770   To which town did Eddie and Marion Yeats move when they married?

771   What is the name of Chalkie Whiteley's grandson?

772   To which country did they emigrate?

773   Who was the grandson's grandmother on the other side of the family?

774   What was the name of Ken Barlow's first girl-friend?

775   Who put a sea-lion in Jack and Annie Walker's bath?

776   What was Albert Tatlock's favourite drink?

777   What was Albert awarded in the First World War?

778   What rank did he hold in the Army?

779 Who was Elsie Tanner's second husband?

780 How did he die?

781 At which number in the street did Elsie live?

782 What was the name of Ivy Tilsley's husband?

783 Who unsuccessfully opposed Renee Bradshaw's application for an off-licence for the corner shop?

784 What was the name of the bookie with whom Blanche Hunt moved to Kenilworth?

785 With whom did Jed Stone lodge?

786 Who played Leonard Swindley?

787 In which subject did Ken Barlow graduate?

788 What was Hilda Ogden's maiden name?

789 Who is the ex-girlfriend by whom Mike Baldwin has a son?

790 What is the name of the son?

992 **I had minor roles in *Dr Who* and *The Jewel in the Crown* before becoming *EastEnders'* nastiest nasty.**

791 Which female character appeared in the first episode but has never appeared since?

792 Of what did May Hardman die?

793 Who rebuilt no. 7, Coronation Street, after it collapsed in 1965?

794 Jack Duckworth (seemingly in the doghouse again) is Bet's cellarman at the Rover's, but which brewery supplies the pub with its beer?

795 Of what misdemeanour did the brewery suspect Billy Walker just before he left the Rover's for the last time, giving up the licence?

796 What is Percy Sugden's job?

797 Who was Kevin Webster's girlfriend before Sally, the girl he married?

798 What business did Audrey Roberts conduct for a short time in her front room?

799 With whom did Alan Bradley two-time Rita Fairclough?

Brookside

800 To what substance was Nicholas Black addicted?

801 What was his job?

802 What was the name of his first wife?

803 Who was their daughter?

804 Which resident of the Close did she date?

805 Where did the Collins family live before moving to Brookside Close?

806 At the time of their move, from what job had Paul Collins been made redundant?

807 What is Billy Corkhill's trade?

808 From what job is Harold Cross retired?

809 What was the name of his late wife?

810 Who did the catering at her funeral reception?

811 Who became Harold Cross's lodger?

812 What was the name of the lodger's late wife, who was never seen in *Brookside*?

813 Who was shot dead in a gun siege in the Close?

993 I played Inga Olsen in *Coronation Street* 18 years before becoming boss of a Midlands motel in another serial.

814 What was her job?

815 What was the name of Pat Hancock's girlfriend who lived with him in the house in which the siege took place?

816 From which city did she originate?

817 Who temporarily replaced her in the house?

818 What was her job?

819 What is the name of the local pub?

820 With whom was Sheila Grant drinking at the pub shortly before she was raped?

821 With whom did she share a taxi after leaving the pub?

822 What was the name of his late wife?

823 For what did Damon Grant register after leaving school?

824 For what type of firm did he work?

994 I became producer of *Crossroads* after eight years of producing *The Archers*.

825 From which university did Pat Hancock graduate?

826 In which subject did he graduate?

827 What was his job when he moved to the Close, in 1984?

828 What was the name of the celebrity who opened the Alder Hey Children's Hospital Fête in the summer of 1985?

829 How many times was Heather Haversham married?

830 What were the names of her husbands?

831 From whom did she break off her engagement in 1985?

832 With whom did Matty Nolan have an affair?

833 Who was imprisoned after being framed on a charge of conspiracy to commit a crime?

834 What was the name of his wife?

995 **I play a character who was a great pal of Dan Archer. We went through the First World War in the 5th Borsetshires.**

835 His wife had two sisters. What were their names?

836 How did the elder of the two sisters die?

837 Who was the younger sister's boyfriend in the serial?

838 Why did they split up?

839 What was the name of the married man with whom Lucy Collins had an affair?

840 What is the name of Doreen Corkhill's mother?

841 Which television pop show presenter appeared in *Brookside* and was interviewed by Karen Grant for a student newspaper?

842 Another woman comes between Terry Sullivan and Pat Hancock. This time she is married and Pat met her at a football training session. what is her name?

843 What was the name of Ralph Hardwick's friend whom Harold Cross originally met through a 'lonely hearts' column?

844 Which former Brookside actress starred in the film *Letter to Brezhnev?*

845 What was the name of the character she played in *Brookside*?

846 Who was the character's husband, who died?

847 What was the name of Terry Sullivan's girlfriend after Michelle Jones?

848 With whom did Karen Grant share a flat?

849 Who had the idea of a 'naughty night nurse' kiss-agram service?

Emmerdale Farm

850 What is Mrs Bates' forename?

851 What was her husband's name?

852 What was his job?

853 What are the names of Seth and Meg Armstrong's two sons?

854 What is the name of the local newspaper?

855 Who is Beckindale correspondent?

856 What is his mode of transport?

857 What are the names of the Rev. Donald Hinton's son and daughter?

858 What are the names of Sandie Merrick's parents?

859 What are the names of Jackie Merrick's parents?

860 Which *Emmerdale Farm* actress played Julie Shepherd in *Crossroads*?

861   What is the name of the character she plays?

862   What is the name of this character's son?

863   What is the name of the actress who plays Kathy Bates?

864   What relation is Kathy to Mrs Bates?

865   What was the name of the church warden and Women's Institute member whose husband died in 1972?

866   How did Pat Sugden die?

867   What is the name of the actress who played her?

868   What relation was she in real life to Clive Hornby, who plays Pat's widower Jack Sugden?

869   What job did Joe Sugden take after returning from France?

870   What was the name of Joe's ex-wife, from whom he is divorced?

996   Switching from acting to writing, I created *Coronation Street* and wrote the first 12 episodes.

871   What was her maiden name?

872   Of whose murder was Matt Skilbeck acquitted?

873   What was the name of Annie Sugden's husband?

874   What is Alan Turner's job?

875   What was Henry Wilks' job before he moved to Beckindale?

876   What is the name of the actor who played Tom Merrick?

877   What was Merrick jailed for?

878   Actor Johnny Caesar wrote a hit single, 'Come Home, Rhondda Boy', for Tom Jones in 1981. Which *Emmerdale Farm* character did Caesar play?

879   Which *Emmerdale Farm* actor once played the kilted Jamie in *Dr Who*?

997   **I play a teenager, son of an electrician, and I've joined the police force.**

880 What is the name of the character he plays in the serial?

881 Who was seriously injured when his motorcycle was in an accident with Alan Turner's car?

882 What is the name of the real-life village that provides the setting for the fictional Beckindale?

883 Actor Al Dixon, who died in 1986, played a silent role in *Emmerdale Farm* for six years. What was the name of the character?

884 Which *Emmerdale* actor played Dr Rennie in *Emergency – Ward 10*?

885 What is the name of his *Emmerdale* character?

886 Jackie Merrick was engaged to a nurse. What was her name?

887 Of what nationality was she?

888 One *Emmerdale Farm* actor has a sheep farm in West Yorkshire. Who is he and what is the name of the character he plays?

998 **Years after playing a newspaper delivery boy in a long-running serial, I rejoined it as a youth who became a car mechanic and married a girl called Sally.**

889 What is this character's trade?

890 Who took over as boss of Hotten Market in 1986?

891 Happy days down on the farm for Annnie Sugden, sons Joe and Jack, and Matt and Dolly Skilbeck. But what was the name of Annie's late father (centre)?

892 Which *Emmerdale Farm* actor played Roger Wade in *Coronation Street* in 1965?

893 Which character wrote a book called *The Field of Tares*?

894 Who was Matt Skilbeck's first wife?

895 What relation was she to Annie Sugden?

896 How did she die?

897 What was the name of the nurse who cared for Bella Ryland before she died?

898 Which *Emmerdale Farm* actor, who plays a punk in the serial, appeared in the film *Looks and Smiles*?

899 Who created *Emmerdale Farm*?

999 In 1987 I took over the role of a character who has problems adapting from city life to rural ways.

900 Who built the Colby house?

901 Of what violent act did Sable Scott accuse Jason Colby?

902 To which foreign city did Franky Scott consider moving?

903 What are the names of Jason's children?

904 What was Bliss's connection with Shaun?

905 Who plays Monica Colby?

906 Who previously owned the Titania record company?

907 To whom did the owner sell the company?

908 From which chronic disorder did Fallon Colby suffer?

909 What is the name of Jason's lawyer?

910 By what other name did Fallon call herself?

911 Who raped Fallon?

912 Which two Colbys are twins?

913 Who shot Sable Scott?

914 Why did Franky Scott divorce her husband?

915 What was the name of her ex-husband?

916 What is the name of Sable's art gallery?

917 Who is Jackie Devereaux's real father?

918 What is the first name of the blind musician who released a pop record?

919 How did Monica Colby crash her aeroplane?

920 What was Fallon Colby's maiden name?

921 Who plotted to take over Jason's company?

922 What is Franky Scott's full surname?

923 Where did Fallon and Jeff Colby honeymoon?

WHO AM I?

1000 **I played barmaid Julie in *The Archers* before becoming the daughter of a motel boss in a television serial.**

924 What did a fortune-teller predict Fallon's first child would be?

925 What is the name of Jeff and Fallon Colby's son?

926 What type of car does Miles Colby drive?

927 How were Jason and Connie Colby related?

928 What is Dominique's club called?

929 Who bid against Sable Scott for a rare painting at an auction?

930 Why did Connie Colby hire a detective to follow Sable?

931 Who is Zack Powers' nephew?

932 Who plays Neil Kittredge?

933 Whose portrait hangs on the wall of the staircase in the Colby house?

934 Whom did Sable accidentally run over in her car?

1001 **The character I play is a partner in a Yorkshire pub and has a grandson called Niccolo.**

935 Who is said to be Jeff's father?

936 Which character, played by an actress who is also a singer, appears regularly in both *Dynasty* and *The Colbys*?

937 Who persuaded Jason not to throw Sable out of his house?

938 Who was most against Sable living in the same house as her?

939 What is that character's full forename?

940 Who became involved in a massive bar brawl?

941 Where did Miles Colby propose to Channing Carter?

942 What is the name of Channing's uncle?

943 What stopped Shaun and Bliss Colby from eloping?

944 With whom did Monica have an unexpected affair?

945 What is the colour of the lettering on the Titania record company's labels?

DALLAS

1 Southfork.
2 In a helicopter crash in the South American swamps.
3 Colombia.
4 Emeralds.
5 Mark Graison.
6 In a Dallas park.
7 Charlie Wade.
8 Maria.
9 Jenna Wade.
10 Mastectomy.
11 Alcohol.
12 Cliff Barnes.
13 Lucy Ewing.
14 EWING 6.
15 Bobby Ewing.
16 Kristin Shepard, JR's mistress.
17 Sister.
18 Student doctor.
19 Mitch Cooper.
20 Valentine's Lingerie.
21 Mandy Winger.
22 To break up JR's relationship with Mandy Winger.
23 Ray Krebbs.
24 Jamie Barnes.

25 Jack.
26 In a rock fall while she was mountain-climbing in Mexico.
27 Christopher.
28 Bobby Ewing.
29 Kristin Shepard.
30 B.D. Calhoun.
31 Willard Barnes.
32 Digger.
33 Alcohol.
34 Pamela and Cliff.
35 Southworth.
36 Jason Ewing.
37 Miss Ellie.
38 Amanda Ewing.
39 She went insane.
40 She told him she was pregnant.
41 'Digger' Barnes.
42 Jeff Gray.
43 Los Angeles.
44 Dusty Farlow, Clayton's son.
45 Bobby.
46 Following an accident, he lost the use of his legs and became impotent.
47 Texas.
48 Jenna Wade.
49 In the shower.
50 Sam Culver.
51 Politician.
52 Cancer.

53 Deaf children.
54 Ray Krebbs had a criminal record.
55 She suffered a nervous breakdown.
56 Fashion design.
57 Wentworth Tool & Die.
58 As a comedian on American television.
59 *The Eagle Has Landed.*
60 Barbara Geddes Lewis.
61 1922.
62 *Panic in the Streets.*
63 A model.
64 Howard Keel.
65 Jenilee Harrison.
66 Steve Forrest.
67 A barbecue.
68 William Smithers.
69 Ray Krebbs.
70 Divorce papers.
71 He inherited Jamie Ewing's 10 per cent of Ewing oil shares.
72 Afton Cooper.
73 Singer.
74 Washington DC.
75 To further her political career.
76 Sly.
77 Gary and Valene Ewing.
78 *Knots Landing.*
79 He began building a new house.
80 Charlie Wade.
81 The Oil Barons' Ball.
82 Cliff Barnes.
83 She was a cousin.
84 She found a medal on his desk that had belonged to Jock.
85 To train horses.
86 B. D. Calhoun.
87 Corpus Christi, Texas.
88 Cancer.
89 Jeremy Wendell and JR Ewing.
90 She had no friends in Dallas.
91 John Ross.
92 His stetson.
93 Micky Trotter.
94 Texas.
95 1978.
96 Patrick Duffy.
97 *Wogan.*
98 Donna Krebbs and Cliff Barnes.
99 Mary Martin.
100 The Oil Barons' Club.

Take the High Road

101 Glendarroch.
102 Don Houghton.
103 The Glendarroch estate.
104 Max Langemann.
105 Frederick Jaeger.
106 Kentucky bourbon with ice.
107 To pay death duties.
108 Loch Lomond.
109 Luss.

110 19 February 1980.
111 Peter Cunningham.
112 Sarah.
113 Kay Grant.
114 Rev. Gordon Cockburn.
115 Rev. Ian McPherson.
116 Murdering his mistress.
117 Maggie Ferguson.
118 Alan McIntyre.
119 Douglas Dunbar.
120 McEwan.
121 In childbirth.
122 Nephew.
123 Dougal Lachlan.
124 Graeme B. Hogg's.
125 To investigate the estate's efficiency.
126 Majorca.
127 Teri Lally.
128 David.
129 Highland Games Day.
130 Crofter.
131 Morag Stewart.
132 Lamont.
133 Alcohol.
134 To try to separate her from her boyfriend.
135 Florence Crossan.
136 Laura Ashley.
137 Carol McKay.
138 Ruari Galbraith.
139 Brian and Isabel Blair.
140 Eddie Ramsay.

141 Nephew.
142 Janice Gifford.
143 Malcolm Ryder.
144 To collect the insurance money.
145 By poisoning her.
146 South America.
147 Sarah Jane.
148 Daughter Jill and her then husband Stan Harvey.
149 Rosemary.
150 Sarah Alexander.
151 Annette André.
152 Venice.
153 Meg Richardson, Jill's mother.
154 A Guy Fawkes' Night fire burned it down.
155 A wartime bomb exploded.
156 Tunisia.
157 Alice.
158 Barnaby Blake.
159 Assistant to the hall porter.
160 John Line (Stephen Fellowes).
161 Cook.
162 Start a chicken farm.
163 Anne-Marie Wade.
164 Lois Angell.
165 Hugh Mortimer.
166 He had a fatal heart

attack while in captivity.

167 Hawkins.
168 To become a singer.
169 Rev. Peter Hope.
170 Ruth Bailey.
171 Hugh Mortimer.
172 To marry Jane Templeton.
173 The late John Bentley.
174 Manslaughter.
175 Mavis.
176 Sam Benson.
177 Mrs Meacher.
178 Susan Hanson.
179 Diane Hunter.
180 John Latchford.
181 John Latchford.
182 David Jason.
183 He was on a Youth Training Scheme.
184 Stan Harvey, her ex-husband.
185 A brain tumour.
186 In a fire in Spain.
187 John Crane.
188 He committed suicide.
189 Stan Harvey.
190 Electrician.
191 Waitress Sandra Gould.
192 Paul Greenwood.
193 Diane Keen.
194 General manager.
195 Vince Parker.
196 Postman.
197 Nicky.
198 Frank Adam.
199 America.

200 Roy Mollison.
201 Pneumonia.
202 Farmworker.
203 Angela Kelly.
204 Journalist.
205 Glenda Brownlow.
206 Maureen Flynn.
207 Maureen was killed on the way to the ceremony.
208 Gambling.
209 Kate Hamilton.
210 Anthony Mortimer.
211 Stepbrother.
212 Matthew.
213 Chris Hunter.
214 He interrupted a wages snatch.
215 Lynda Welch.
216 His ex-wife Rosemary.
217 She was jealous of his engagement to Barbara Brady.
218 By a car in a hit-and-run accident.
219 Katy-Louise.
220 She was a test-tube baby.
221 *The Midland Road*.
222 Mary Wilson, wife of the then Prime Minister Harold Wilson.
223 Carlos Raphael.
224 Shughie McFee.
225 Dee Hepburn.
226 Anne-Marie Wade.
227 Roy Lambert.
228 Motel garage mechanic.

229 Daniel Freeman.
230 Stepson.
231 Diane Hunter.
232 He was the victim of a hit-and-run accident.
233 Three.
234 Financial adviser to Hugh Mortimer.
235 Hall porter.
236 Newcastle upon Tyne.
237 Waitress.
238 Philip Goodhew (Daniel Freeman).
239 Mr Darby.
240 Tracey.
241 Mickey Doyle.
242 Jill Chance.
243 Lorraine Baker.
244 Chalet maid.
245 Ron Brownlow.
246 To work on an oil rig.
247 Joanna.
248 Roy Lambert's shop.
249 Jason Hathaway.
250 He fired stones from a catapult at it.
251 Moses.
252 Daniel Freeman.
253 Make public some videotapes showing her as a Bunny girl.
254 The Earl of Wilminster.
255 Maggie Bristow.
256 George-André Arnaud.
257 Elaine Paige.
258 Bomber.
259 Terence Rigby.

DYNASTY

260 Dex Dexter, Blake Carrington and Cecil Colby.
261 Her daughter, Amanda Carrington.
262 She knew that he was dying and would leave her a large inheritance.
263 La Mirage.
264 Alexis.
265 Ben Carrington.
266 The pipeline deal.
267 Rita.
268 Australia.
269 Alexis.
270 Christina Carrington.
271 Claudia.
272 Claudia was lighting candles and a curtain caught alight.
273 On a boat.
274 Blake Carrington's chauffeur.
275 Fallon Colby.
276 The *Denver Mirror*.
277 He lied when he told her that he had been married before.
278 Jessica.
279 Jackie Devereaux.
280 Garrett Boyston.
281 Sammy Jo Carrington.

282 Rock Hudson.
283 AIDS.
284 A horse.
285 Rita, the woman who impersonated Krystle Carrington.
286 His mother, Emily Carrington.
287 Danny.
288 *The Colbys*.
289 Denver Carrington.
290 Denver Colby.
291 To put Alexis out of business.
292 Sammy Jo Carrington.
293 Stepmother.
294 Sister.
295 Venezuela.
296 Caracas.
297 Five years.
298 She wrote a book about Alexis' life.
299 England, at a boarding school.
300 The Carlton.
301 Alexis.
302 Alexis and Krystle Carrington.
303 Dominique Devereaux.
304 La Mirage.
305 Claudia Blaisdel.
306 Doctor.
307 Niece.
308 Delta Rho.
309 She bred horses.
310 Brown and white.
311 Dex Dexter.
312 John Forsythe.
313 Denver, Colorado.
314 Los Angeles.
315 Luke Fuller.
316 Moldavia.
317 The king of Moldavia.
318 Semi-paralysis.
319 Photographer.
320 Ali MacGraw.
321 Michael, Blake Carrington's chauffeur.
322 Christina Carrington.
323 George Hamilton.
324 Krystle (Carrington).
325 Dex Dexter and Clay Fallmont.
326 Kate O'Mara.
327 Wear make-up or wash her hair: she said someone in jail would not look like a top model.
328 Blake Carrington.
329 So that she could testify against Ben Carrington in a court case over the La Mirage fire.
330 Clay Fallmount.
331 On a tennis court.
332 Ben Carrington.
333 Pamela Sue Martin.
334 Reporter.
335 From her blue eyes.
336 A plot of land, the main feature of which was a large crater.
337 Jaguar.
338 Alice.
339 Ben Carrington.
340 At the bottom of her champagne glass.

341 In an attic at the Delta Rho ranch.
342 Sammy Jo.
343 Steven Carrington.
344 Cassie.
345 Murder and arson.
346 $10,000.
347 Michael Nader.
348 Michael Praed.
349 1933.
350 *The Stud* and *The Bitch*.
351 Nolan Miller.
352 Linda Evans.
353 *The Last Frontier*.
354 Gordon Thomson.
355 Zack Powers.
356 Peter Holm.
357 John Forsythe.
358 His secretary/personal assistant, Dana.
359 Adam Carrington.

The Archers

360 Borsetshire.
361 The *Borchester Echo*.
362 Home Farm.
363 Manor Court.
364 Gyp.
365 He failed to hit a fox.
366 Jack Woolley.
367 The Borchester Press.
368 The Am.

369 October 1980.
370 80.
371 Trying to lift a sheep.
372 Shires.
373 The Cat and Fiddle.
374 Caroline Bone.
375 With the death of Grace Archer.
376 Bird-watching.
377 Late seventeenth century.
378 Ambridge Hall.
379 Kenton.
380 Sophie Barlow.
381 Haydn Jones.
382 One of Marjorie Antrobus' Afghan hounds.
383 St Stephen.
384 Col. Freddie Danby.
385 Neil Carter.
386 The SDP.
387 Country-and-western music.
388 Jean-Paul.
389 The Snells.
390 Gwen Berryman.
391 Duckingham Palace.
392 Walter Gabriel.
393 A door-stop.
394 Brookfield.
395 Lettie Lawson-Hope.
396 Lakey Hill.
397 Walter Gabriel.
398 Linda Snell.
399 John Archer.
400 Frank Middlemass.
401 A smithy.
402 John and Nelson Gabriel.

403 Forrest.

404 William and Lisa Forrest.

405 17 December 1920.

406 The Cricklewood Sidings robbery.

407 Walter Gabriel.

408 The Borsetshires.

409 Tony and Pat Archer.

410 Patrick Lichfield.

411 Martha Woodford.

412 Sid Perkins.

413 Polly.

414 In a road accident.

415 Squire John Lawson, also known as 'Mad Lawson' or 'Black Lawson'.

416 On Heydon Berrow.

417 HRH Princess Margaret.

418 Norman Painting.

419 Matthew Thorogood.

420 Dr McLaren.

421 Manorfield Close.

422 Kitchen maid at the Manor House.

423 Public school.

424 Grey Gables Country Club.

425 Rats.

426 'Barwick Green'.

427 Nigel Pargetter.

428 Hollerton Junction.

429 Grace Archer.

430 In a stable fire.

431 Bill Insley.

432 Mr Snowy.

433 Pilot in the Canadian Air Force.

434 Lilian.

435 Its 35th birthday.

436 Dolly Tredgold.

437 For being sick into the piano.

438 Brian Aldridge.

439 Betty Tucker and Dorothy Adamson.

440 Walford (E20).

441 Silk Cut.

442 Pauline Fowler (actress Wendy Richard).

443 Pete Beale.

444 Joseph and Mary.

445 Pete and Kathy Beale's home.

446 The BBC's Elstree studios in Hertfordshire.

447 Julia Smith.

448 Asthma.

449 'Every Loser Wins'.

450 18.

451 The Queen Victoria.

452 Jane How.

453 The Kick.

454 Vodka, gin, brandy, whisky and Grand Marnier liqueur.

455 The Samaritans.

456 Den Watts.

457 Roly and Willy.

458 Nick Cotton.

459 Albert.
460 Saed.
461 Kathy and Pete Beale.
462 His father died of lung cancer.
463 He stole it from the Christmas Club.
464 James Willmott-Brown.
465 Arthur Daley (of *Minder*).
466 Tom Watt.
467 Pat.
468 Dot.
469 He stole her cheques and cashed them.
470 The local register office.
471 Orient Express.
472 Philip.
473 AIDS.
474 For killing a taxi-driver.
475 The Banned.
476 'Something Outa Nothing'.
477 Pam St Clement.
478 They are twins.
479 Pete Beale's brother Kenny.
480 Scotland.
481 He was killed by a lorry while trying to save a child from being run over.
482 Purple.
483 'Drop dead.'
484 The name has never been revealed.
485 Annie.
486 That he could get her into bed.

487 Arthur Fowler.
488 Turkish.
489 Hassan.
490 Cot death.
491 Burglary.
492 Eight years.
493 By sending taxis on false calls.
494 OzCabs.
495 01-503 5577.
496 Terminal cancer.
497 Nejdet Salih (Ali Osman).
498 Simon.
499 The Isle of Wight.
500 Angie Watts.
501 Trinidad.
502 Health visitor.
503 She fell down the stairs and broke her hip.
504 Charlie.
505 Shoplifting.
506 Harold.
507 'Anyone Can Fall in Love'.
508 Angie.
509 Angie.
510 Neville.
511 72.
512 Sharon Watts.
513 The menopause.
514 Pauline Fowler.
515 She was still in love with Den.
516 Den.
517 Pills and alcohol.
518 Her cousin Rezaul.
519 Prostitution.
520 Prostitutes.

521 Hairdressing.
522 Andy O'Brien.
523 He wanted the band to play the song he had composed and was refused.
524 Tomato juice.
525 The community centre.
526 Barry Clark.
527 Youth Training Scheme.
528 A bra.
529 Knitting.
530 Dot Cotton.
531 Naima Jeffery.
532 Mark Fowler.
533 He had never had a regular girlfriend.
534 Roly.
535 He was Asian.
536 He overheard her drunken conversation with a barman on the Orient Express.
537 A Walkman.
538 Her father's records.
539 Personnel officer in the City.
540 Italian.
541 Naima's shop.
542 Tony Carpenter.
543 Cassie.
544 He stripped down to his underpants and jumper and washed his clothes in the machines.
545 Pauline Fowler and Dot Cotton.
546 Dot.
547 Gatecrash.

548 Being over-protective.
549 Ali's Café.
550 Her grandfather's name was Albert; he was named after Prince Albert, who was married to Queen Victoria.
551 May.
552 She saw him giving Michelle money.
553 Graphic designer.
554 Fruit and vegetables.
555 The Dagmar.
556 New Zealand.
557 A stud.
558 A jacket.
559 Growing a beard.
560 Feminism.
561 The Asian Women's Group.
562 Anna Wing.
563 As a co-contractor and woman taxi-driver for female clients only.
564 Sue Osman.
565 A pair of hand-made earrings.
566 Shirley Cheriton (Debbie Wilkins).
567 Victoria Maternity Hospital, Barnet, Hertfordshire.
568 The washing of animals in the machines.
569 He was a market trader.
570 Tony Carpenter.

571 A watch and antique jewellery.
572 War-paint.
573 He had a nervous breakdown.
574 Jane Laurie.
575 Tony Mettale.
576 Nick Berry.
577 Anita Dobson.
578 Letitia Dean.
579 Yellow.
580 Diamond.
581 She is a notorious hypochondriac.
582 Guitar.
583 St Mark's Square.
584 It is real.
585 A skull-and-crossbones.
586 To impress Andy.
587 To read and write.
588 Male.
589 Dot Cotton.

HOWARDS' WAY

590 *Dallas-on-Sea.*
591 Stephen Yardley.
592 Gerry Glaister.
593 Polly and Gerald Urquhart.
594 *The Boatbuilders.*
595 Tarrant.
596 Jack Rolfe.
597 Bursledon, near Southampton, Hampshire.

598 Charles Frere.
599 Claude Dupont.
600 Fashion designer.
601 Sonya Fielding.
602 American.
603 Ken Masters.
604 Charles Frere.
605 Alcoholism.
606 Sonya Fielding.
607 Mother.
608 Claude Dupont.
609 The Jolly Sailor.
610 Amnesia.
611 Ken Masters.
612 'Dear Lord and Father of Mankind'.
613 Maurice Colbourne.
614 Orrin Hudson.
615 She sold it to Orrin's parents.
616 The Mermaid Boatyard.
617 Marti Webb.
618 In his filing cabinet.
619 Dulcie Gray.
620 Her anti-post bet on the horse she owned in the Steward's Cup race failed when the horse went lame.
621 Because she had to sell her house to ease her financial problems.
622 Claude Dupont.
623 *The Flying Fish.*
624 *Barracuda.*
625 Fibreglass.
626 Animal rights.
627 Abi.
628 Abi threatened to

reveal that Charles Frere was her father, which would have ruined his business reputation.

629 Ken Masters.

630 Petrol pump attendant.

631 Goodwood.

632 He was run over by a speedboat while water-skiing.

633 At Jan Howard's fashion show, for which he designed all the clothes.

634 Ken Masters hired a heavy mob to break up Leo's demonstration against development on a nature reserve.

635 *Lynnette*.

636 To stop the Mermaid Boatyard being shut down.

637 Sade.

638 Paris.

639 Southampton.

640 Mechanic at the Blue Bell Garage.

641 Ena Sharples.

642 Joan Walker and Gordon Davies.

643 Doreen Lostock.

644 Maison Valerie, in Rosamund Street.

645 Spiros Papagopoulos

646 Eunice 'La Composita' Bond.

647 Angela Douglas.

648 Christine Hardman.

649 Norman.

650 Martin.

651 In a car crash while serving with the Army in Northern Ireland.

652 Wally Randle.

653 Jenny Bradley.

654 15.

655 Rita Fairclough's.

656 Singing.

657 Terry Duckworth.

658 About £200.

659 Kevin and Sally Webster's party at Mrs Ogden's.

660 Stuart Latham.

661 Patricia Phoenix (Elsie Tanner).

662 The Glad Tidings Mission Hall.

663 Ena Sharples.

664 Violet Carson.

665 Elsie Lappin.

666 Norman.

667 Frank Barlow.

668 HM The Queen and HRH Prince Philip.

669 Weatherfield.

670 Archie Street, in the Ordsall district of Salford.

671 Frank and Ida.
672 Post Office supervisor.
673 Bet Lynch.
674 Baldwin's Casuals.
675 Steve Holt.
676 Martin Shaw.
677 He sold his scooter.
678 Plymouth.
679 Because Mike Baldwin had previously had an affair with Ken's wife Deirdre.
680 Dennis Tanner.
681 Leonard Swindley.
682 Ena Sharples.
683 Elizabeth I.
684 David Barlow.
685 The Duke of Bedford.
686 Plumber.
687 Pneumonia.
688 Andrea Clayton's.
689 Harry.
690 Milkman.
691 Bill Webster.
692 Alcohol.
693 Maggie.
694 Gordon.
695 Betty Turpin, Maggie's sister.
696 Because he was illegitimate.
697 Ron Cooke.
698 Darren.
699 In a car crash in Australia, in 1970.
700 Stan and Hilda Ogden.
701 In the raincoat factory.

702 Deirdre Hunt (now Barlow).
703 Taking part in a banned anti-Vietnam War demonstration.
704 Len Fairclough.
705 Janet Reid.
706 With Valerie's mother, in Glasgow.
707 He was the uncle of Valerie, Ken's first wife.
708 Jerry Booth.
709 Littlewood.
710 Alec Gilroy.
711 Roy Barraclough.
712 Manager of the Graffiti club.
713 Neil Crossley.
714 Terry.
715 The Western Front.
716 A photographic shop.
717 At the funeral of Ernest's mother.
718 Nugent.
719 Vera Duckworth.
720 The Parachute Regiment.
721 Mawdesley Street.
722 Nellie (*née* Briggs).
723 Stanley.
724 Peter Noone (later of Herman's Hermits).
725 Sharon Gaskell.
726 Brian Tilsley.
727 Inkerman Street.
728 Billy Walker.
729 Bill Gregory.
730 Chief Petty Officer.
731 Colin Appleby.

732 In a car crash.
733 Frank Barlow.
734 Concepta (*née* Riley).
735 Christopher.
736 Lucille Hewitt.
737 Cleaner at the Rover's.
738 Of a heart attack in the Rover's snug.
739 Blanche Hunt.
740 Ray Langton.
741 Len Fairclough's secretary.
742 Janice Stubbs.
743 Tenant.
744 Henry Wakefield.
745 19 Inkerman Street.
746 The Mark Brittain Warehouse.
747 Jerry Booth.
748 Assistant at the corner shop.
749 Harriet.
750 Three.
751 Phyllis, Renee and Audrey.
752 Mother.
753 Potter.
754 Ena Sharples.
755 Alfred.
756 Ian Latimer.
757 Australia.
758 He believed Gail was pregnant by Ian.
759 Tricia Hopkins.
760 The Mark Brittain Warehouse.
761 Jim's Café, in Rosamund Street.
762 Beaumont.
763 Clitheroe.
764 Derby.
765 Her daughter Joan.
766 Chalkie Whiteley.
767 Debbie.
768 West Germany.
769 Seddon.
770 Bury, Lancs.
771 Craig.
772 Australia.
773 Phyllis Pearce.
774 Susan Cunningham.
775 Dennis Tanner.
776 Rum.
777 The Military Medal.
778 Lance Corporal.
779 US Army Master Sergeant Steve Tanner.
780 He was murdered by another soldier.
781 No. 11.
782 Bert.
783 Annie Walker.
784 Dave Smith.
785 Minnie Caldwell.
786 The late Arthur Lowe.
787 History.
788 Crabtree.
789 Maggie Dunlop.
790 Mark.
791 Elsie Lappin (actress Maudie Edwards), who handed over the corner shop to Florrie Lindley.
792 A heart attack.
793 Len Fairclough.
794 Newton and Ridley.
795 Selling supermarket

spirits instead of the
brewery's.

796 Community centre
caretaker.
797 Michelle Robinson.
798 Hairdressing.
799 Gloria Todd.

Brookside

800 Heroin.
801 Local government
architect.
802 Barbara.
803 Ruth.
804 Rod Corkhill.
805 The Wirral.
806 Industrial production
manager.
807 Electrician.
808 Train driver.
809 Edna.
810 Annabelle Collins.
811 Ralph Hardwick.
812 Grace.
813 Kate Moses.
814 Nurse.
815 Sandra Maghie.
816 Glasgow.
817 Gill Beaconsfield.
818 Probation officer.
819 The Swan.
820 Alun Jones, her part-
time course tutor.
821 Matty Nolan.

822 Teresa.
823 Youth Training
Scheme.
824 Painters and
decorators.
825 Nottingham
University.
826 Food technology.
827 Hospital porter.
828 Russell Grant.
829 Twice.
830 Roger Huntington
and Nicholas Black.
831 Tom Curzon.
832 Mo Francis.
833 George Jackson.
834 Marie.
835 Petra Taylor and
Michelle Jones.
836 She committed
suicide.
837 Terry Sullivan.
838 She was having an
affair with her dance
teacher, Richard de
Saville.
839 James Fleming.
840 Julia Brogan.
841 Paula Yates.
842 Andrea Parkin.
843 Madge Richmond.
844 Alexandra Pigg.
845 Petra Taylor.
846 Gavin Taylor.
847 Vicki Cleary.
848 Guy Willis.
849 Pat Hancock.

Emmerdale Farm

850 Caroline.
851 Malcolm.
852 Schoolteacher.
853 Jimmy and Fred.
854 The *Hotten Courier*.
855 Amos Brearly.
856 Bicycle.
857 Clive and Barbara.
858 Tom Merrick and the late Pat Sugden.
859 Jack Sugden and his late wife Pat.
860 Jean Rogers.
861 Dolly Skilbeck.
862 Sam.
863 Malandra Burrows.
864 Daughter.
865 Annie Sugden.
866 In a car crash.
867 Helen Weir.
868 Wife.
869 NY Estates regional manager.
870 Christine.
871 Sharp.
872 That of Harry Mowlam.
873 Jacob.
874 NY Estates manager.
875 He ran a Bradford wool mill.
876 Jack Carr.
877 Poaching.
878 Bill Middleton.

879 Frazer Hines.
880 Joe Sugden.
881 Jackie Merrick.
882 Esholt, in Yorkshire.
883 Walter.
884 Richard Thorp.
885 Alan Turner.
886 Sita Sharma.
887 Indian.
888 Peter Alexander (Phil Pearce).
889 Builder.
890 Eric Pollard.
891 Sam Pearson.
892 Frazer Hines (Joe Sugden).
893 Jack Sugden.
894 Peggy.
895 Daughter.
896 In childbirth.
897 Nan Wheeler, her cousin.
898 Tony Pitts (Archie Brooks).
899 Kevin Laffan.

The Colbys

900 Jason's grandfather.
901 Pushing her down the stairs.
902 Singapore.
903 Miles, Monica, Bliss and Jeff.
904 He was her boyfriend.

905 Tracy Scoggins.
906 Dominique Devereaux.
907 Zack Powers.
908 Amnesia.
909 Garrett Boyston.
910 Randel.
911 Miles Colby.
912 Miles and Bliss.
913 Jason Colby.
914 She was in love with Jason.
915 Philip Colby.
916 The Colby Collection.
917 Garrett Boyston.
918 Wayne.
919 It ran out of fuel.
920 Carrington.
921 Zack Powers.
921 Scott Colby Hamilton.
923 Rio.
924 A girl.
925 LB.
926 Porsche.
927 They are brother and sister.
928 Dominique's.
929 Zack Powers.
930 She suspected Sable of having an affair with Zack Powers.
931 Shaun Powers.
932 Philip Brown.
933 Sable Scott's.
934 Connie Colby.
935 Cecil.
936 Diahann Carroll.
937 Miles, Bliss and Monica Colby.
938 Franky Scott.
939 Francesca.

940 Miles Colby.
941 On a merry-go-round.
942 Lucas Carter.
943 They saw on television that Miles Colby was in serious trouble.
944 Neil Kitteredge.
945 Red.

946 Elaine Paige.
947 Jean Alexander (Hilda Ogden in *Coronation Street*).
948 Simon May and Leslie Osborne.
949 Caroline Ashley (*Take the High Road*).
950 Alan Rothwell (Nicholas Black in *Brookside*).
951 Hugh Manning (Rev. Donald Hinton in *Emmerdale Farm*).
952 Ross Davidson (Andy O'Brien).
953 Maurice Colbourne (Tom Howard).
954 Mary Crosby (Kristin).
955 Stephanie Beacham (Sable Scott).

956 Tony Adams (Adam Chance in *Crossroads*).

957 Wendy Richard (Pauline Fowler).

958 Malandra Burrows (Kathy Bates in *Emmerdale Farm*).

959 Barbara Bel Geddes (Miss Ellie).

960 Jane Rossington (Jill Chance in *Crossroads*).

961 Tracey Childs (Lynne Howard).

962 Jane Hutcheson (Sandie Merrick in *Emmerdale Farm*).

963 Alison Dowling (Elizabeth Archer in *The Archers*, Lisa Lancaster in *Crossroads*).

964 Linda Gray (Sue Ellen in *Dallas*).

965 Pamela Vezey (Kath Fellowes in *Crossroads*).

966 Susan Tully (Michelle Holloway in *EastEnders*).

967 Diana Davies (Mrs Bates in *Emmerdale Farm*).

968 Charlton Heston.

969 Donna Reed.

970 Patricia Shakesby.

971 Vivien Heilbron.

972 Sheila Mercier (Annie Sugden in *Emmerdale Farm*).

973 Doreen Sloane (Annabelle Collins in *Brookside*).

974 Jan Harvey (Jan Howard).

975 Kathy Staff (Norah Batty in *Last of the Summer Wine*).

976 Noele Gordon, Roger Tonge and Jane Rossington, who played Meg, Sandy and Jill Richardson in *Crossroads*.

977 Tony Anholt (Charles Frere).

978 Dee Hepburn (Anne-Marie Wade in *Crossroads*).

979 Anita Dobson (Angie Watts in *EastEnders*).

980 Priscilla Beaulieu Presley (Jenna Wade in *Dallas*).

981 Charles Collingwood (Brian Aldridge).

982 Lynne Perrie (Ivy Tilsley in *Coronation Street*).

983 Graham Seed (Charlie Mycroft in *Crossroads*).

984 Joan Collins (Alexis Colby in *Dynasty*).

985 Betty Alberge.

986 Patrick Duffy (Bobby Ewing in *Dallas*).

987 Phil Redmond.

988 Bill Kenwright.

989 Jenilee Harrison.

990 Catherine Oxenberg (Amanda Carrington).

991 Tony Hatch.

992 Leslie Grantham (Den Watts).

993 Gabrielle Drake (Nicola Freeman in *Crossroads*).

994 William Smethurst.

995 Chriss Gittins (Walter Gabriel in *The Archers*).

996 Tony Warren.

997 Jason Hope (Rod Corkill in *Brookside*).

998 Michael Le Vell (Kevin Webster in *Coronation Street*).

999 Ewen Emery (Willie Gillespie in *Take the High Road*).

1000 Kathryn Hurlbutt (Debbie Lancaster in *Crossroads*).

1001 Arthur Pentelow (Henry Wilks in *Emmerdale Farm*).